750

D1456992

COLLECTION

PRIVÉE

COLLECTION

PRIVÉE

70 Images Illustrating
the Comité Colbert
and the Art de Vivre

Texts by
JEAN-JACQUES ABLY

English version
Deirdre Engel

COMITÉ COLBERT

Conception, réalisation : Arbook International

The human soul is the battleground of the eternal conflict between poetry and prose. Each one of us, deep down, aspires to an ideal. Some, the happy few, find solace in religion, art or science. But for the rank and file, those of us who are not Saint Theresa, Newton or Gauguin, there is only one means of gratifying our yearning for perfection, and that is by trying, in our own small way, to enhance the quality of our everyday lives.

It is an all-out battle against the prevailing forces of ugliness and gloom, and we fight on with unweakened resolve – though we have to confess to receiving a helping hand, without which the battle would surely be lost, from a small brotherhood of samourais whose mission is to come to our aid in keeping the encroaching enemy at bay. We shall not offend their modesty by naming them, for their in some cases centuries-old fame has spread to the four corners of the earth. They are the businessmen, designers and craftsmen who have made the luxury industry what it is today – in France, where we can truly say, without undue chauvinism, that it is on its home ground. And 1954 witnessed the founding of the COMITE COLBERT, comprising seventy of the greatest names in French luxury goods, to act as their ambassador and advocate, and defend their interests in the noblest sense of the term.

Everyone knows that a prima donna is composed of a lady who sings and a husband who will do his utmost to give her the support she needs. By placing itself at the service of the finest quality French craftsmanship, the COMITE COLBERT is, as it were, the prima donna's husband. Its ultimate aim, in addition to its legitimate financial and commercial concerns, is to see the blossoming of good taste and art de vivre across the globe and so relieve the grayness that is our daily lot. The raison d'etre of the COMITE COLBERT, its distinction, we might say, lies in enabling us all to share with the great Edith Piaf a glimpse of *la vie en rose* and so enjoy the taste of sheer poetry.

♦ HAUTE COUTURE ♦

The figure of the seamstress strikes a sympathetic chord in the more literary among us, taking us back to Zola's modest little dressmaker's apprentice straining her eyes over a fine seam in the dim glow of an oil lamp. The world of what we now know as fashion designing is quite a different matter. Here we enter the realm of "high" fashion, where the *couturier* is always *grand* and *couture* is by definition *haute*. Gone, too, are the days of women's hold over the profession – now they simply don't have a look in. Paradoxically so for haute couture is a universe created exclusively for women, it not by them. The male of the species is expected to go out and tinker with his car while madame performs the rituals associated with that peculiar calling of hers — to do her utmost to look pleasing to herself so as better to appeal to others. Henry de Montherlant disrespectfuffly maintained that there is no distress so dire that a woman cannot get over by going out and buying a new dress. Well, that's all to her credit. It proves that women do not brood. It also goes to show that, haute couture can look forward to a bright future. Too bad for all those, prince consorts and gallant escorts who will grow old in their walk-on parts. There is no immediate likelihood that the *beau* seen in the company of some celebrated high priestess of elegance will receive much more attention than the delivery boy bringing flowers to the door.

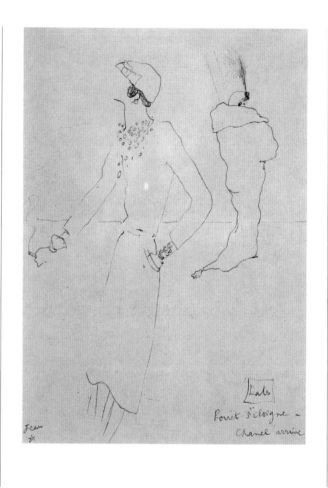

"Poiret s'éloigne.
Chanel arrive" by Jean Cocteau. 1928. Lithograph.

"MISS DIOR"
BY GRUAU. 1949. GOUACHE.

Audrey hepburn
IN THE FILM *ARIANE* DRESSED BY HUBERT DE GIVENCHY. 1956.
PHOTOGRAPH: RAYMOND VOINQUEL.

HAUTE-COUTURE

DESIGN, SPRING/SUMMER 1989. LONG DRESS WITH LAYERED
TAFFETA SKIRTS AND TULLE "POINT D'ESPRIT". WATERCOLOR.

HAUTE-COUTURE

DESIGN; SPRING/SUMMER 1986. PHOTOGRAPH: SARAH MOON.

H AUTE-COUTURE
DESIGN, FALL/WINTER 1988-1989 BY MARYLL LANVIN.
MARKER DRAWING.

"LÉONARD AIME
LÉONARD". DRAWING BY VAN HOVE FOR DANIEL
TRIBOULLARD. 1987. LITHOGRAPH.

DRAWING BY
P. LOUCHEL FOR THE PARISIAN MAGAZINE *LA FEMME CHIC*. 1944.

Haute-couture
DESIGN FALL/WINTER 1952-1953. DRAWING BY GRUAU. INK WASH.

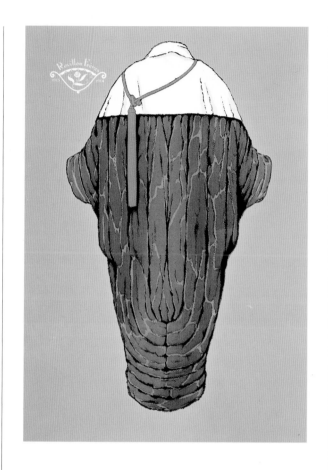

D ESIGN
1913-1914 LITHOGRAPH

Style maketh man, so the saying goes,
and the conscientious egotist is wont to
turn this (misquoted) proverb to his own
account by asking himself not the question of all questions "Who am I?" but
"What is my style?" or, more to the point,
"How good is my style?" Well, dear
egotist, your style is as good as the con-
tents of your pockets or the accessory
under your arm. Your belongings speak
for you. And beware, for the slightest
faux pas in this domain can be fatal. A
favorite game played in the subway or
bus is to guess at the personality of
fellow-passengers just by looking at their
shoes. Well, this sartorial semiology (!) is
not confined to footwear. A man's way
of knotting his necktie speaks volumes

about him, as does his pen or cigarette lighter. The leather his belt or pocket-book are made of is the absolute yard-stick of his taste. He may even be for-given his unsavory habit of chewing gum if the said gum is plucked from a custom-designed crocodile-skin case. His obses-sion for sightseeing will be overlooked at the mere sight of the traditional crafts-manship of his luggage. And so on.

Objects are not slaves, they are merely possessions, but everybody is well aware that to have is to hold. And to hold one's own in this world one must uphold its finer achievements, so as to be able to go through customs declaring only the excellence of one's suppliers and rous-ing a cheer of admiration.

Drawing carried
out by Georges Lepape for the 1926 Hermès catalogue.
Pen and ink wash.

Shirt created by
M. RENÉ LACOSTE IN 1933. PHOTOGRAPH: IRVING PENN. 1986.

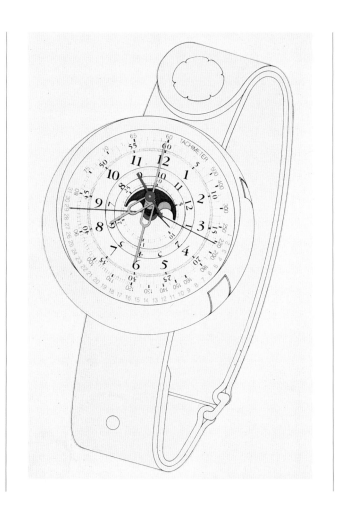

<small>S</small>TUDY FOR THE
WATCH DESIGNED BY GAE AULENTI. 1988. LINE DRAWING.

STUDY FOR
FOUNTAIN PEN BY GINA BRUZZI. 1989. PEN AND INK.

◆ PERFUMES ◆

So much has been said and so much written about perfume, with the eloquence that only the intangible, the unfathomable can inspire. Its poetic and literary associations have been cited, as have the stirrings of nostalgia it kindles within us; Proust's memory of the senses have been quoted and Baudelaire's verse recited. Sociologists have remarked on the curious, if not to say extraordinary, phenomenon of an industry and a trade built up, literally, on thin air – fragrance is a product that has no physical reality. The human nose, to be sure, is real enough. Even the most carefully selected of fragrances cannot prevail over a cold in the head. If the man in the street may be permitted to put in a word, let it simply be said that this insubstantiality does have a highly practical side to it in the world today — it cannot be taken away from you. In these troubled times, even the least brave at heart can safely walk the streets, be it in the most dubious part of town, swathed in a cloak of the most heady and priceless of scents. However opulent that mantle may be, however sumptuous the aura surrounding our scented stroller, that unseen, ethereal adornment will be secure from prying hands, and the wearer, light as air, can enjoy the luxury of a prized possession unmolested. Perfume is such stuff as dreams are made on. With perfume our fancy takes flight, and this is half the secret to happiness.

CARON

"LA BOUTIQUE
MONTAIGNE", IN PARIS, BY PIERRE LE TAN. 1986. PEN AND
INK WITH WATERCOLOR.

"N₀5"
BY SEM. 1921. LITHOGRAPH.

"Eau sauvage".

1988. PHOTOGRAPH: DOMINIQUE ISSERMANN.

" Ysatis"

ILLUSTRATION BY PIERRE COULON, 1984. AEROBRUSH.

"VOL DE NUIT"
ILLUSTRATED BY DARCY. 1933. ADVERTISING.

Studies
OF BOTTLES AND POWDER BOXES FOR FITTED CASES.
1929/1930. WATERCOLOR.

Reproduction of the
Boat-shaped bottle *NORMANDIE*, originally created in
1935 for the liner's maiden voyage to New York.
Photograph: Fabrice Corny.

THE LANVIN
SYMBOL INSPIRED BY THAT OF PAUL IRIBE. 1926. LITHOGRAPH.

"Cœur-Joie",
FIRST FRAGRANCE BY NINA RICCI ILLUSTRATION BY CHRISTIAN
BÉRARD. 1946. GOUACHE.

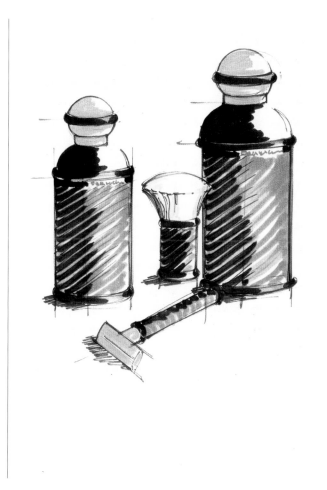

"FRENCH LINE":
STUDIES BY JOËL DESGRIPPES. 1984. MARKER.

"FEMME"
FRAGRANCE CREATED IN 1944 BY MARCEL ROCHAS
AS A WEDDING PRESENT
FOR HIS WIFE HÉLÈNE. ADVERTISEMENT.

♦ JEWELRY ♦

What kings, emperors, religious leaders and women – all the beings who have you on your knees – have in common is that not only do they reign supreme but they possess that extra something that catches your romantic fancy – they love a challenge. And what gives a woman the ascendancy over her peers in that august assembly, drawing from us more gasps of wonder than even the sweet fragrance of her hair or the satin bloom of her skin, is her ability to rise to a challenge not by marching into battle or leading a crusade but by wearing jewelry as though to the manner born. The foe may be less daunting, but it takes no small amount of pluck to sally forth arrayed in pearls or diamonds or to launch

out across a crowded room with a dia-
dem poised upon your brow — and the
effect may be no less devastating.

"Behold these jewels upon my head and
these gems at my throat. They are the
most priceless accomplishments of human craftsmanship. There are those who
would sell their soul to possess them. I
am simply content to wear them. But in
doing so, I have at heart that your gaze
should linger in wonder on my person,
not their fiery luster. Would that you
were blinded only by the radiant splen-
dor of my inner charms."

"That will be easy, madame; for nothing
can surpass the talent of your jeweler,
other than the miracle of your smile. And
then, your wish is my command."

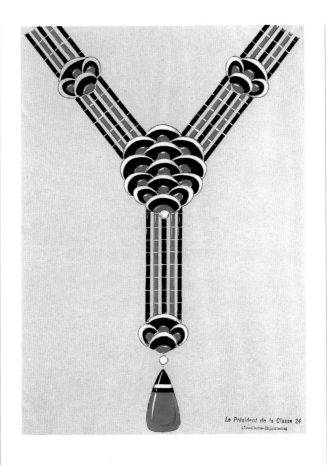

Le Président de la Classe 24
(Joaillerie-Bijouterie)

DRAWING OF A LONG
NECKLACE CREATED FOR THE DECORATIVE ARTS EXHIBITION.
1925. GOUACHE.

CONSTANT FORCE
MECHANISM. PEN AND INK WITH WATERCOLOR BY LOUIS
ABRAHAM BREGUET. 1818.

Sketches
OF PLATINIUM PENDANT NECKLACES SET WITH BRILLIANT-CUT
DIAMONDS, CREATED FOR THE
"SALON DES ARTISTES DÉCORATEURS" IN 1931. GOUACHE.

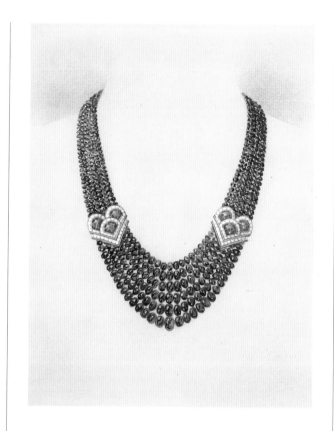

E MERALD
NECKLACE BELONGING TO THE ''DIAPHANES'' COLLECTION.
1986. GOUACHE.

"DEUX PLUMES" PIN, GOLD
WITH "INVISIBLE-SETTING" RUBIES, GIVEN
BY KING EDWARD VIII TO Mrs WALLIS SIMPSON IN 1936.
GOUACHE ON RHODOÏD.

♦ DECORATION ♦

For centuries, and often from father to son, designers and decorators have had the answer to the profoundest metaphysical question of all. They are living proof that God exists and that there is no need to go looking for Him way up in heaven or in the celestial accents of a Gregorian chant. God is within us – or at least in those of us who are not content with the furnishings and fittings that pass muster with the common mortal, but are inhabited by the desire to live surrounded by beautiful things. There is a price the discerning have to pay to indulge their esthetic sense. How easy it would be to live within four concrete walls, on a floor of beaten earth – but no, the true connaisseur will put every ounce of his energy, thought and talent into gracing his interior with nothing less than the best in fine furnishings and objects.

Such attention to detail cannot be explained away by the mere desire to impress. It is a matter of self-esteem and an intuitive knowlege of what is best for one, coupled with the need to live up to an ideal. These finer feelings presuppose that one has a soul – and a soul is something we would call by a different name if it were not intrinsically divine in character. This is what we have set out to prove. And should any argument be adduced to prove the contrary, what does it matter? Who cares whether we are right or wrong? What counts is that there are things to embellish our lives, and people to produce those things.

"PERSANE"

BY BEZOMBES. 1968. LITHOGRAPH.

Sɪʟᴠᴇʀ

CANDLESTICK HOLDER CREATED BY E.A. CHARLES. 1930.

GOUACHE.

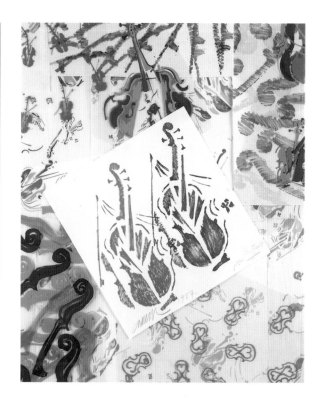

Studies by
ARMAN FOR A PRINTED FABRIC. 1987.

STUDY FOR A
HANGING LAMP DESIGNED BY HENRY DELISLE FOR AN IMPERIAL
CASTLE AT ST. PETERSBOURG. 1904. WATERCOLOR.

Scheme for
THE RUSSIAN BAR LEDOYEN IN PARIS DESIGNED BY JACQUES
GRANGE. 1988. GOUACHE AND COLORED INK.

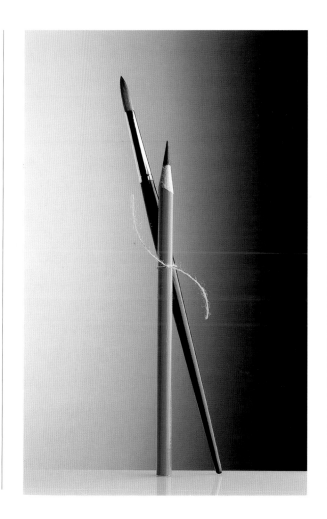

"MANUEL CANOVAS,
CRÉATEUR TEXTILE". POSTER FOR THE EXHIBITION AT THE
"MUSÉE DES ARTS DE LA MODE".
PARIS 1986. PHOTOGRAPH: DANIEL JOUANNEAU.

"Vendanges":
PREPARATORY DRAWING. 1986. GOUACHE ON VELLUM.

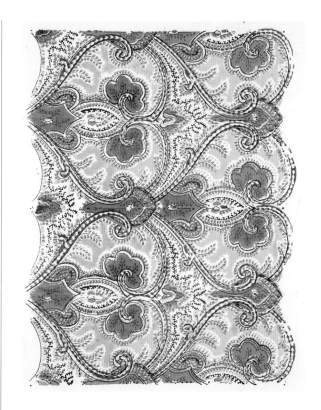

Fabric printed
ACCORDING TO AN 18th CENTURY PATTERN.

♦ ARTS DE LA TABLE ♦

One of the most potent though least
known thinkers of our century, the
philosopher Albert Caraco, once uttered
these thought-provoking words, to be
found in a recent guide to table manners:
A fine meal which is not a moment of the
mind is like wild beasts closing in on the
kill. Feeding ourselves does at times
bring out the beast in us. The remedy is
only partly to be sought in the virtues of
dinner-table conversation, which has an
uncanny knack of gravitating towards the
latest Current Event. Nor should we set
too much store by the special brand of
humor of the resident wit, which is liable
to fall flat at the crucial moment. Better
to trust to an elegantly laid table, a daz-

zling white cloth, gleaming silverware, dainty porcelain and sparkling crystal. This is what will stand the best chance of conjuring up the *moment of the mind* so dear to our philosopher.

The makers of fine tableware put all their artistry into creating the effect that a magnificent display can have on a gathering, so as not to rouse the glutton that is said to lurk in each and every one of us. And this is how those who grace our tables with their fine wares have contributed over the ages to what we call civilization, making History something more than a riotous round of junketing, and enabling us to seat the Brummels and the Byrons around our table. Hats off to those who have accomplished so awesome a feat.

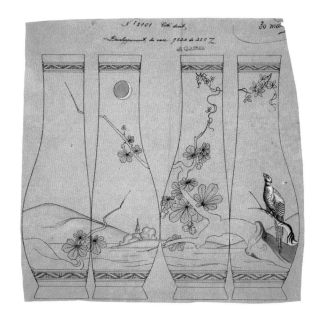

Rᴇᴘʀᴇsᴇɴᴛᴀᴛɪᴏɴ
OF A VASE DECORATION OF JAPANESE INSPIRATION. 1986.
GOUACHE AND INK WASH ON VELLUM.

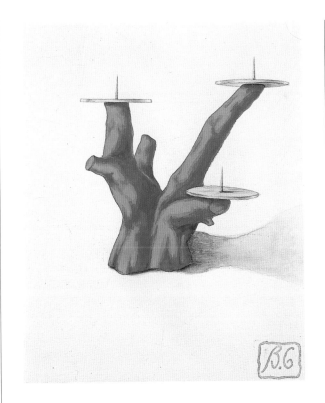

"TRAPANI",
DESIGNED BY ELIZABETH GAROUSTE AND MATTIA BONETTI.
1989. WATERCOLOR.

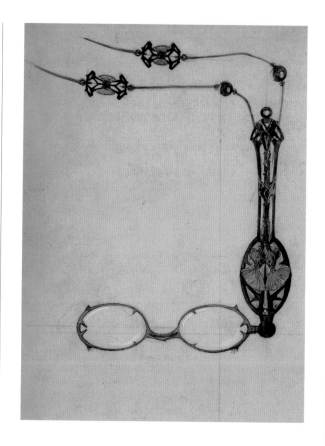

D ESIGN OF LORGNETTE
WITH A THISTLE PATTERNED CHAIN RENÉ LALIQUE.
1902/1903. GOUACHE ON PARCHMENT PAPER.

SHEET
OF TECHNICAL DRAWINGS. CREATED BY JOSEPH BLEICHNER. 1933.

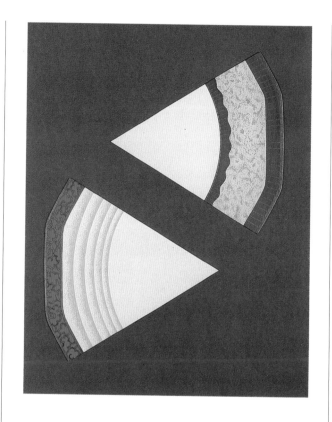

S TUDY FOR DINNER
PLATES BY JEAN HAMIET DESIGNED FOR THE EXPOSITION DES
ARTS DÉCORATIFS. 1925.

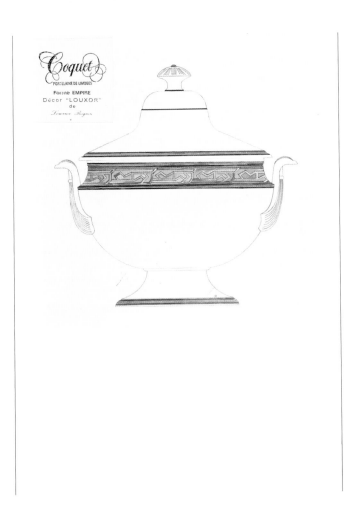

"L OUXOR"

DESIGNED BY LAURENCE BRIGNON. 1987. WATERCOLOR.

"Palais d'été : décor
marronnier". From the handpainted catalogues. 1897.

Studies for the
COLORING OF PLATES "ROSEBUD". 1928. WATERCOLOR.

"Reflets"
1983. PHOTOGRAPH: JEAN-LOUP SIEFF.

Porcelaine
COVERED VASE ON BRONZEBASE. 1880. WATERCOLOR.

SILVER AND GLASS
VASE WITH BLACK MARBLE BASE DESIGNED BY JEAN PUIFORCAT.
1934. WATERCOLOR.

"When pirates, Bacchus, made so bold / As to defy you, so we're told, / They so provoked your heav'nly ire / That, vengeance-bent on that sad crew, / You ordered as chastisement dire / That water'd ever be their brew", It was the 17th century poet and wit Saint-Amant who penned these lines. Nowadays, a part from the odd athlete or waistline-watcher, only ducks will openly admit to taking to water. There is of course nothing wrong with having a drink of water. But everything has a purpose. Water brings refreshment to the body. Wine provides sustenance to the soul. And let's drink — as should be our maxim in all things — not because we need to but for the pleasure of it. Should our thirst be quenched, then a glass of cognac or champagne will be the answer. And as we sip it, let our minds wander to all those rows of bottles lying there expectantly in their fine coating of venerable dust – their very existence tells us how necessary is the superfluous. It is no accident that our language has but one word – *spirit* – to denote both the breath of the divine and the liquid produced by distillation. In the exhilaration we feel when we partake of fine wines or spirits – provided it does not exceed the bounds of decency – it is as though we were receiving a gift from heaven, a token of divine benevolence towards us. What else is it but Bacchus smiling down on us from Mount Olympus and sending us a foretaste of the nectar of the gods?

ONE OF
THE LABELS USED IN THE 19TH CENTURY.

PHOTOGRAPH: JEAN LARIVIÈRE. 1987.

M ENU
"SPORTS AND LEISURE" DRAWN BY SYLVESTRE. 1911.

Advertisement. 1920. Lithograph.

Reproduction
OF AN ALPHONSE MUCHA POSTER FROM BEFORE 1900.

"L E LIVRE".
1986. PHOTOGRAPH : JEAN LARIVIÈRE FOR VOGUE.

"CHAI 2000":
ARCHITECT RICARDO BOFILL. PHOTOGRAPH: K. TAHARA. 1988.

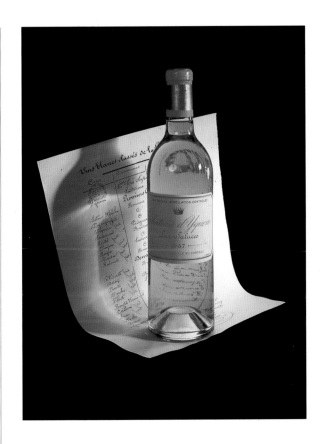

"ONE NEEDS NO LESS
THAN SEVEN VINES AND FOUR LONG YEARS OF CONSTANT
CARE TO PRODUCE ONLY ONE BOTTLE
OF CHÂTEAU D'YQUEM". 1973. PHOTOGRAPH: JACQUES VARGUES.

Luftschiff Deutschland.

Speisen

Bester Beluga-Malossol	Port. Mk.	4.—
Russ. Kaviar-Import-Haus Berlin, Joh. Kaius, Boll.		
Franz. Masthuhn, 12—14 Mk.	" "	3.—
Straßburger Gänseleber-Pasteten	" "	3.—
Salate	" "	1.—
Erdbeeren nach Melba	" "	3.—

Weine

1908er Rauenthaler Berg	Mk.	4.50
Boll. Wilh. Ruthe, Wiesbaden		
1905er Steinberger, Originalabfüllung	"	8.—
Boll. Wilh. Ruthe, Wiesbaden		
Moseltreppchen	"	4.—
Mach. Berkmann, Creppchen-Kelterei, Köln		
1898er Ducru Beaucaillou	"	6.—
J. Bundorf, Wichelhausen & Co., Bremen		
Burgeff grün	"	8.—
G. H. Mumm, Reims, gout americain	"	17.—
Courvoisier Cognac *** p. Glas	"	1.—

Fahrt von Friedrichshafen nach Stuttgart
Baden-Baden, Frankfurt und Düsseldorf
: : : : : : : April 1911 : : : : : : :

Ernst Kölblin, Hofbuchdruckerei, Baden-Baden

"ZEPPELIN" MENU
OFFERED TO PASSENGERS OF THE AEROSTAT IN GERMANY.
1911. WATERCOLOR BY PLASMAN.

LOUIS XIII DECANTER
MADE OF BACCARAT CRYSTAL CONTAINING COGNAC AGED
MORE THAN 50 YEARS. 1989. PHOTOGRAPH: DANIEL
JOUANNEAU.

♦ HOTELS, RESTAURANTS, ♦

♦ GASTRONOMY ♦

It is truly regrettable that every country's Bill of Rights does not include a provision for all citizens to be granted the right to spend twelve months of their lives staying only in luxury hotels, dining only in the best restaurants and partaking only of the finest foods – and be given an allowance for doing so. This sabbatical year, in the proper sense of the term, would give every human being a glimpse of happiness, which is just as crucial to an understanding of the world as the veneer of culture acquired at school, for a dose of respectable epicureanism is well worth a smattering of trigonometry when it comes to facing life's tribulations. But to come down to earth, how agreeable it is to find that, in a world bereft of the joys of the transatlantic steamer and the Pullman car, the specialists whose profession it is to provide a haven of comfort to the traveler and cater to the delights of the palate continue, as though of a common accord and often in one and the same place, to live up to their tradition of excellence. What a pleasure it is, not only for one's own well-being but for the experience of meeting those who frequent such places! There are no beings so genial as the *habitués* of grand hotels and the top league of fine food stores. Luxury is second nature to them; they are past masters at the art of simplifying life rather than littering it with the superfluous. There is a lesson in wisdom to be learnt from them, which makes it such a subtle pleasure to be in their company.

THE BRISTOL
AT THE OPENING IN 1924. PHOTOGRAPH: DRAEGGER.

Menu

ILLUSTRATED BY SONIA RYKIEL. 1987. PENCIL.

"Le printemps"
THE HOTEL AS SEEN BY PIERRE PAGÈS. WATERCOLOR.

SUITCASE

LABEL (COLLECTION LOUIS VUITTON).

SUITCASE
LABELS (COLLECTION LOUIS VUITTON).

"LA DORADE
EN CROÛTE DE SEL". RECIPE HANDWRITTEN IN THE STYLE OF
THE "REVOLUTION", 1989.

"A L'AMI
THUILLIER" BY JEAN COCTEAU. 1959. PENCIL.

"N EW
LOOK HÉDIARD". LABEL.

" THE PARTY"
ILLUSTRATION OF THE "FÊTE GASTRONOMIQUE" BY ANDRÉ
FRANÇOIS, 1987. PEN AND INK WITH PASTEL.

THE COMITÉ COLBERT

BACCARAT 1764

BERNARDAUD 1863

CHAMPAGNE BOLLINGER 1829

BOUCHERON 1858

BREGUET 1775

BUSSIÈRE ARTS GRAPHIQUES 1924

CARON 1904

CHANEL 1912

PARFUMS CHANEL 1924

CHARLES 1921

CHÂTEAU CHEVAL BLANC 1832

CHÂTEAU LAFITE-ROTHSCHILD 1855

CHÂTEAU D'YQUEM 1786

CHRISTIAN DIOR 1947

PARFUMS CHRISTIAN DIOR 1948

CHRISTOFLE 1830

COQUET 1963

COURVOISIER 1835

D. PORTHAULT 1924

DAUM 1875

DELISLE 1895

DIDIER AARON 1923

ORFÈVRERIE D'ERCUIS 1867

FAÏENCERIES DE GIEN 1821

GIVENCHY 1951

PARFUMS GIVENCHY 1957

GUERLAIN 1828

GUY LAROCHE COUTURE 1957

HÉDIARD 1854

HERMÈS 1837

PARFUMS HERMÈS 1948

HÔTEL DE CRILLON 1909

HÔTEL GEORGE V 1928

HÔTEL LE BRISTOL 1923

HÔTEL PLAZA ATHÉNÉE 1911

HÔTEL ROYAL ÉVIAN 1909

JEAN PATOU 1919

PARFUMS JEAN PATOU 1925

JEANNE LANVIN 1889

CHAMPAGNE KRUG 1843

LA CHEMISE LACOSTE 1933

LALIQUE 1910

PARFUMS LANVIN 1925

CHAMPAGNE LAURENT-PERRIER 1812

LENÔTRE 1957

LÉONARD 1943

CHAMPAGNE LOUIS ROEDERER 1776

LOUIS VUITTON 1854

MANUEL CANOVAS 1963

MAUBOUSSIN 1827

MELLERIO DITS MELLER 1613

RESTAURANT HÔTELLERIE MICHEL GUÉRARD 1965

NINA RICCI 1932

PARFUMS NINA RICCI 1945

OUSTAU DE BAUMANIÈRE 1945

PIERRE BALMAIN 1945

PIERRE FREY 1935

PUIFORCAT 1820

RÉMY MARTIN 1724

REVILLON 1723

PARFUMS REVILLON 1937

ROBERT HAVILAND & C. PARLON 1924

ROCHAS 1925

CHAMPAGNE RUINART 1729

CRISTALLERIES DE SAINT LOUIS 1767

SOULEÏADO 1780

S.T. DUPONT 1872

VAN CLEEF & ARPELS 1906

CHAMPAGNE VEUVE CLICQUOT PONSARDIN 1772

Membres associés :

MANUFACTURE NATIONALE DE SÈVRES 1738

LA MONNAIE DE PARIS 1552

ORCHESTRE NATIONAL DE FRANCE/ADEMMA 1925

THÉÂTRE NATIONAL DE L'OPÉRA DE PARIS 1669

List of members as of January 1st 1989.

Achevé d'imprimer
sur les presses d'I.G. Castuera S.A.
à Pampelune, juin 1989
Photogravure Prodima S.A., Bilbao